*All proceeds will benefit Eagle Acres Ministries.*

# SEASONS;
## Finding God Wherever You Find Yourself

Roxanne Meeuwsen, MA

*Eagle Acres Ministries*

Scripture quotations, unless otherwise noted, are taken from the New King James Version. Copyright ©1979, 1980, 1982 by Thomas Nelson, Inc. Used by permission. All rights reserved.

Scripture quotations marked (NLT) are taken from the Holy Bible, New Living Translation, Copyright ©1996. Used by permission of Tyndale HousePublishers, Inc., Wheaton, Illinois 60189. All rights reserved.

Scripture quotations marked (NIV) are taken from the HOLY BIBLE, NEW INTERNATIONAL VERSION. NIV. Copyright ©1973, 1978, 1984 by International Bible Society. Used by permission of Zondervan Publishing House. All rights reserved.

The accounts of individuals and families are accurate, but most of the names and places have been changed.

**Seasons**
Copyright ©2009 by Roxanne Meeuwsen, MA
All rights reserved.

**ISBN: 978-0-557-16645-9**

Eagle Acres Ministries
Printed in the United States of America

***I dedicate this book to all my precious family.***

*Heavenly Father, thank you for always loving me and carrying me through every season I go through. May this work be used for Your glory alone.*

*Greg, besides our Lord, you are my very best friend. I can't see myself succeeding in anything without my hand in yours.*

*Kids, you have taught me and helped me more than I can ever adequately thank you for…I hope you know how dear you are to dad and I, truly loved.*

*Mom, Dad, and Amy, thank you for always believing in me and for being excellent teachers. I love you like crazy.*

*My Dear spiritual family at City Gate Church, thank you for your support and steadfast encouragement. You are such a blessing to me, and you are so dearly loved.*

## Thank You

*To family and professional friends who have given me honest feedback and helpful review for this project: Gregory Meeuwsen, Patricia Stokley, Nancy Miller, Pastor Taunja Hoole*

*To Nancy Miller for her stellar editing services and to the Miller family for their extreme generosity. Without their amazing encouragement, this project would still be a dream.*

# Introduction

Well, I was going to wait until the house was clean before I started writing. I was going to finish putting away the decorations from the last holiday and make sure I had a nice cozy place all set up to write. I was going to clear my schedule for a few days, as much as a mother of five can clear her schedule. I was even going to make a cup of hot tea before I started my first book. Hot tea just seemed like a good idea. I mean don't all good writers need to sip on tea, sit back in a comfy environment, and look out a big picture window for a few moments as they write their great pearls of wisdom from the Lord? I'm serious. This must be how it works!

A few moments ago, it dawned on me, that I have fantasized about and romanticized this moment for so long that if I continued on the same path for much longer, I may never get started at all. You see, the house will always need to be a little cleaner. My "cozy place" may never be just right, and tea certainly cools down quickly, doesn't it? Sometimes I sit down to gaze out that picture window for a moment only to notice that I haven't tended properly to the weeds just outside. Often, I try to find a cozy corner in my house and I discover that it has been a long time since anyone has dusted around the edge of the candlestick holders.

    Well, it's time to stop dreaming about doing what I've been longing to do. It's time to write the books that God has laid on my heart. The children are still awake. The men in my husband's Bible study group are just in the next room. The Christmas decorations are still up and New Years day has come and gone. There is even dust on my computer screen. I feel that God wants me to start now though. He is speaking to my heart tonight. I must write without tea!

# Preface

*Dad said we could do it and I believed him! After all, I had been his assistant for years as we swapped out break pads, put in new shocks, CV boots, and alternators. It was easy. He'd ask for a 7/16 box end and I'd find it right where it was supposed to be in the big red and chrome Craftsman toolbox. He'd ask me to help bleed the brakes and I knew just how long it would be before he'd say, 'let her up.'*

*We worked well together. He liked his shop kept neat and organized. I liked to feel needed and industrious. It made sense. We could put a clutch in my Subaru over Christmas break. I was home for three weeks before I had to head back to the college. That was plenty of time to rest, celebrate, and get the job done! Dad was going to save me a ton of money. I knew he could do it. He was a good mechanic and I was blessed!*

*After celebrating Christmas, we got anxious to start the difficult job. We made sure we had all the parts we needed and we hooked up an engine hoist from the ceiling of the garage to help with the heavy lifting. I was feeling pretty confident as we took the hood off of the car and set it against the far wall. I was even fine when dad took out two large bins and told me that they were for the parts we were going to remove. It took us nearly two entire days to tear the engine out, undoing all sorts of hoses and clamps and wires in the process. I had never seen him put a clutch in before. I didn't realize this was such a complicated procedure.*

*At some point, I started to panic and crazily began labeling everything that came off of the vehicle. I tried to do it without dad noticing so that I wouldn't hurt his feelings. I quickly wrote masking tape labels like 'left side by radiator' or 'middle back 2 hoses, 1 long, 1 short, clamp tight.' At one point my father noticed and smiled at me. I admitted what I was doing and he said, 'good idea. There are a lot of things to keep straight.' This is when I started a full blown organizational system putting all parts in order of how they came off, with their hoses next to them.*

*The garage looked like an old junk yard for several days. Then dad was ready to take off the driver's side door. This really freaked me out. I whined to the Lord that I really needed that car. He had given it to me and now it was gone forever. We'd NEVER get it to run again. I started thinking about how drastically my life would have to change. I'd have to find a ride to church now rather than being the one* picking up people along the way. I'd have to cancel this, and what about that? I had come to <u>need</u> a car in my life. What was I going to do?

I never had to find out. Several hours after the door came off, the door went back on. Then, one by one, every last piece of the torn apart Subaru was reassembled. It ran and ran well, for many more years!

I'll never forget how hopeless it felt to look around that cluttered garage. It was a horrible feeling, a feeling that I never had to experience if I had only kept my focus where it needed to be. When my focus was on my father, the mechanic who could help me, I was at peace. When I chose to focus on the disarray around me, I quickly grew overwhelmed.

*When my focus is on my circumstances, I can't see Jesus.*

## When I look Up

On my left side, there's a mountain.
I can barely see the top.
If I tried to climb it,
I know I'd have to stop.

On my right side, there's an ocean,
Screaming out at me.
I could never cross it.
The water's much too deep.

In front of me is a raging storm.
Behind me is a desert wide.
A wall of fire surrounds me Lord.
There's nowhere I can hide.

But when I look up, When I look up,
I know that my eyes,
are where they're supposed to be.

When I look up, When I look up,
My circumstances are no longer all I see,
When I look up.

For when I look up, Oh Lord, I see You.
And fear leaves my heart.
When I look up I see, what You want me to be,
and I have a brand new heart, when I look up.

It is my desire that in the soon coming days, you will determine what season(s) you are in. It is my hope that you will discover what events and whose hands brought you to the place you find yourself. It is my prayer that you will find joy, hope, and purpose right where you are, while looking forward to the next seasons the Lord has planned for you!

# A Season of Apples

# Chapter One

*When a grown man sits and waits for God to move in a specific way in his life, thinking his life will then begin, he often misses out on what God is currently doing all around him. He is so content in dreaming of what will be, that he does not notice what is. Unbeknownst to him, it is often the simple blessings all around him, the daily chain-breaking and captive-freeing miracles that make and lead up to the move of God that he longs to see. For now, he is content to wait. He has seen God move in mighty ways in the past. He knows in his heart that God can move again. He is looking for something similar to what he's seen before. It is all he knows. He can't trace the hand of the Lord right now. He doesn't know what God is up to. One day soon though, the man will recognize the truth. God has been moving all along.*

Seasons are something we can all relate to. There are the seasons of the year: winter spring, summer, and fall.

There are seasons of life: infancy, childhood, youth, and adulthood. There are seasons to many things, even apples. My favorite fruit starts as a seed, then goes through many seasons, such as dormancy, germination, and growth, eventually becoming a tree. The tree goes through even more seasons before an apple finally appears! Spiritually speaking, seasons are periods of time where we have experienced specific patterns. These are patterns in our walk with God involving areas such as our attitudes, feelings, behaviors, and emotions. Some seasons are relatively short, lasting only as long as they take to identify and to confront. Other seasons last or seem to last a lifetime.

In the Fall of 2004, I received an answer to prayer that changed my life. It helped me look at life differently than I ever had before. I began to recognize my life as a series of seasons.

It was a cold, rainy October afternoon. I had worked only half a day that Friday. I wanted to stop by the grocery store, get home, and clean house before the kids returned home from school and the weekend started.

*We like weekends to be all about family time whenever possible. School and work demand a great deal of our attention during the week, as do many of our other responsibilities. The weekends are a time when our family gets to just "hang out" for a while! We love spending time together doing silly little things.*

*Last weekend we made a little boat of wood and cork and floated it down the stream in our pasture land. The whole family footed out to see the expedition. We cheered when it floated! The water wasn't quite deep enough to make it all across our land, but it has been raining all week! I've never seen the kids so excited about rain! I'm sure more boating adventures are on the horizon!*

Well, I had quite a grocery list for the store that week. I ran out of budgeted money before I ran out of items on my list. I tried to be wise, deciding what was important and what was 'fluff.' I quickly decided that fruit was 'fluff.' I had a pantry full of canned fruit. I did not need fresh fruit for the fruit bowl. Half the time I wound up tossing out an old orange or banana anyway. Fruit could wait until next time.

Quite pleased with myself for sticking to our budget, I hurried home to put away groceries and mop the floor. As I was mopping the floor, my headache returned. I vacuumed the entire house and put the kitchen rugs back down on the newly dried floor. My migraine was even worse now. I tried to think of other things as I dusted, but the pain made me nauseous. I quietly prayed that God would heal me and take away the headache, but I continued to hurt. As I started to unload the dishwasher, I looked out my kitchen window in tears, locking eyes with Heaven. I prayed a prayer of desperation, deep from my heart. It went something like this.

**Lord,**
**I know you can see me. I know you can hear me. You are always faithful to my family. I've seen you do so many amazing miracles. God, You've**

even saved my very life.....But I'm really, really discouraged right now. I've been battling these headaches for a long time, Lord. The pain pills are expensive. I don't have any right now. We're trying to pay off the bills from my surgery Lord. We paid our tithe first. We've tried to help others as you've led us to. Now, I need your help, Lord. I can't do this anymore. I'm so tired of being in pain.

I've been praying for Sam and Maddie, Lord, and I don't see you moving. They're still getting divorced. Why, God? And I've been interceding for others that still seem to be so far away from You. I need to see you move Lord. I need to know You're still listening to me.

I tried to be wise today Lord. I spent only what we had and our fruit bowl is empty. I'm tired of having to choose between fruit and bread God. I'm tired of having to choose between medicine and a telephone. I know I should be thankful for what I have, but these headaches make it hard to be thankful for anything Lord. I need your help. You're the only one who really understands how bad I'm hurting right now.

I'm trying hard not to complain to the rest of the world Lord, but I'm screaming out to You. I wish you would reach down and just pick me up and hold me in your arms. I need to hear your heart beat, with my head on your chest. I need You to wipe away my tears and lift my head toward You. I need for You to tell me that everything is going to be alright, because You hear me and You are here with me through all of this. I'm tired of feeling alone Father. I'm tired of trying to appear strong when I feel so frail.

I know deep inside You care about me. You've shown me countless times in a million ways. I have no idea why my insecurities are so strong right now. I only know that I'm coming to You with them. I feel stupid for breaking down right now, but Lord, I guess I just need to know that You hear what I'm saying and what I am saying matters to You.

I'll trust You even if I don't hear You speak to me Lord. I'll serve You whether or not I feel You are answering me. I'll know You're faithful. I'm not that stupid. You have always been faithful to me. You have saved my life in so many ways. I'll always trust You. Still Lord, I'm asking You to show me that You are hearing me, that You care for me and love me as You always have. I know it's stupid. I sound crazy, but I need to know now.

Lord, that fruit basket is empty. It's not that we need the food. You know we have plenty. I just 'want' fresh fruit Lord. I just want to know that You hear me. Please send me fruit Lord. Please send it before the weekend is done. It's gotta be the craziest thing I've ever asked for Lord. I need to know Lord. I need to know You hear me. Do You hear me? Do my words matter? We all like apples Lord. We all like apples.

    Sometimes when you pray a prayer of desperation, you can feel very foolish. I was embarrassed for praying in such an undignified way, but God knew who I was and He loved me anyway. I cried all the way through my prayer, sobbing hysterically at times. When I was through, I collapsed on the couch for a while. I arose headache free a few moments before the kids got home.

## Chapter Two

Let me tell you a little something about the man I married. First of all, I truly believe that God hand picked him for me. He's Grizzly Adams, Prince Charming, and Bozo the Clown all wrapped up into one! On our first date, instead of roses, he brought me a trunk load of firewood for my fireplace! I'm not kidding! To Greg, that was better than roses and chocolates. He was professing his love by sharing his bounty! Though I did eventually get flowers, I must say I preferred the wood!

My husband has a heart of gold. He loves to help others. He cares deeply for those who are hurting. He knows how to show mercy and he is a wonderful husband and father. With all that said, I thought that if I told him about my prayer for apples, he'd think I was crazy! I told him anyway.

"Honey, my sister's on the phone. She wants to know if we want to come over tomorrow and pick out some pumpkins at the farm," Greg called across the room on Friday night.

"Sure, that's fine." I answered.

"Hey Sweetie?" Greg giggled as he hung up the phone. "Do you think God is sending you pumpkins instead of apples?"

I threw a pillow at my smart mouthed husband and then finally laughed at myself out loud. "I might, in fact, be a little crazy," I thought aloud. The weekend was far from over though and I was going to just wait and see what happened!

I'm sure Saturday was a fine day, but I don't recall much about the morning, except that I looked on the front porch and the back porch when I woke up to make sure someone didn't anonymously make an 'apple drop' in the middle of the night! One might say I was obsessed. Later that day, my husband and I went to town for a little while. I was reluctant to leave, just in case my apples were on the way. Then I got to thinking that there were probably more apples in town than there were up on our hill! On the way back home, driving up the brush-lined gravel road that we share with about a dozen neighbors, out popped a gentleman from the bushes on the right!

We hadn't seen this neighbor in quite a while. In fact, we had only spoken with him a few times in the five years we lived on the hill. However, today, the day after I prayed a fervent prayer for apples, he literally popped out of the bushes on the side of the road. He stopped our car with the wave of his hand.

Greg first noticed his demeanor and smile, his serious, yet gentle eyes. This man reminds Greg very much of his Granddad growing up. I, however, with a huge lump in my throat, noticed the apples in his hand. He came over to my window, which I barely had the strength to roll down. He didn't even look at me. He looked at Greg. They talked about who knows what for five minutes or so. He rarely even looked toward me. Then, the moment I had been waiting for finally arrived. He looked straight into my eyes.

"Want a couple of pathetic looking apples? They're the last ones that the frost didn't get, I reckon." He didn't have to ask me twice!

"Sure. Thanks." He must have thought I was nuts, extremely poverty-stricken, or in some kind of pain, because I couldn't fight back the tears. We left shortly after because Greg knew I was about ready to lose it.

*Have you ever received a gift that let you know that someone was in tune with you, that they were listening to you and understanding you? Have you ever received a gift that made you feel unconditionally, extraordinarily loved? Have you ever wondered briefly about someone's feelings for you, only to be shown in an undeniable way that you were so loved all along? Times all of this by several trillion and you'll understand half of what those apples meant to me that day! God heard me. I knew He did! I couldn't explain it away. It was my miracle. It was just for me. If He heard that prayer, as pathetic as I was being, He heard all my prayers! I already knew He did, but this reminder, these apple shaped love letters proved it to me again!*

I basked in the apple glow the rest of the day! I dreamed of apples that night. I took pictures of the apples from the Lord. I wanted to remember this miracle forever. I decided then and there to decorate my kitchen in apples some day! Greg and I taught an adult Sunday School class. The next morning, we told the class about the story of God's love. The apple story went on and on. The class encouraged each other to trust God with our dreams, our futures, and even our fears. We talked about the importance of giving God the glory for all the wonderful things He does. People started giving us apples.

    I made apple cobblers for several people I had been praying for, especially for people I was greatly burdened for. I made a special cobbler for Maddie, with the apples from the Lord. The apples from the Lord were the sweetest Golden Delicious apples I have ever tasted. I decided I wouldn't eat any more apples until I saw miracles for the people I was praying for. I started seeing a lot of miracles in my life.

## Chapter Three

Before I knew it, Apple Mania had set in! I would be driving down the road, see a stop sign, and be reminded of apples! The thought of apples would fill me up with so much love from God that I could almost burst. I called them my love letters from the Lord. I noticed that traffic signals looked like the Macintosh, the Golden Delicious, and the Granny Smith! I noticed that tail lights and flashing red lights and bottoms of overturned rusty barrels all reminded me of God's love. Soon, friends started delivering me apple gifts!

My wonderful coworker, Nancy, had a special gift of encouragement. She knew exactly when someone needed to be reminded that they are a child of God, and He is the lifter of their head. For a period of several months, Nancy found about every little apple-scented, apple-flavored, apple-filled treasure from here to the other side of the orchard and quietly left it on my desk as a surprise. She wasn't looking for recognition or even for the joy of seeing me smile. She seldom saw me enjoy any of the gifts, as we often worked different hours. Nancy just knew that apples reminded me of God's love and power. What a special friend!

A very special young woman from our church gave me my very favorite apple present the week before Christmas. It was an oil painting that she had done in an art class in high school. The young mother had kept the painting tucked away safely in her closet for many years, not knowing its extreme value or beauty. Even as she handed it to me, she explained that it was her first and only painting, and that it was far from perfect. As I gazed upon the picture, however, I couldn't imagine anything lovelier to display in my home.

The painting held a silver bowl full of golden delicious apples! There was no laced table setting or fall landscape to distract the viewer's attention, just beautiful apples. I saw no flaws. I didn't see the work of an amateur artist. I saw the hand of God leading a high school girl for a moment of destiny ten years down the road. I saw the hand of God intervening in my life long before I ever prayed my prayer of desperation. The verse on the back of the canvas read, *"Timely advice is as lovely as golden apples in a silver basket."* (NLT) Proverbs 25:11

*God may use some tiny, little ordinary event in your life today to significantly, even radically, shake another's world tomorrow!*

*Do you ever wonder if what you are doing right now, this very day, will have any effect on the rest of your life? Do you ever wonder if God can use all the little ordinary, mundane things you do? Jolene might have asked herself, "What difference could a painting make?" Sometimes we spend a great deal of time wondering if and doubting that we'll ever be able to make the contributions to the world that we want to make. It's high time that we step out of ourselves and realize that if God can take dirt and spit and make man, then He can take you and I and do anything He wants to.*

    The apples came. The apples went. We never grew tired of them because a great deal of them seemed to be going through a revolving door. I recall grocery shopping late one night and picking up some apples at the store, along with supplies for making a few cobblers in case the Lord laid someone on my heart. Before I had reached our driveway, I had thought of way more people to pray and bake for than I had apples for.

    "What does this mean Lord? Do I need to go out and buy more apples? I don't understand."

    Then I felt like God was telling me to give the apples away. I had someone burning on my heart that I was to deliver the apples to the next morning.

    "What Lord?" I spoke out loud. "That's crazy. What would she do with a big bag of apples? Did she pray for apples too?"

    I couldn't risk it. I thought I had heard from the Lord, and I had to obey. If I was being asked to help be an answer for another person's prayer, I had to respond. Being seen as foolish was a risk I'd have to take.

My youngest daughter woke up the next morning to see a huge bag of beautiful new apples on the kitchen table. It was like a gift to her for the taking. She knew that apples were blessings from God and she opened the bag to take one to her teacher. She was thinking of taking another for herself when I ran in.

"Don't eat that! They aren't ours," I stammered.

"Well, whose are they mommy?" she asked. I explained that God spoke to me to give the apples to a friend. I said she could keep the one for her teacher, but that we needed to close the rest of the bag back up. Thinking she might be disappointed, I put my arm around her and told her I'd buy some more apples soon.

My sweet little dark-eyed princess looked up at me smiling and said, "Do you think she'll know how much God loves her now?"

"I think she will," I smiled back!

*Sometimes it's very difficult to hear God's voice. Most of the time it's because of the other noises and activities going on all around us. It's not that God is not speaking. It's just that we get so easily distracted and so easily delayed. Sometimes, hearing God's voice isn't the challenge, obeying it is. God sometimes tells us to do things that seem silly or foolish to us. We worry about what others will think. We worry that maybe we haven't really heard God at all. We tell ourselves that God's voice must sound deep, profound, and extremely melancholy. We forget that God inhabits the praises of His people! We forget that God asks us to have faith like a child.*

    I walked up onto an unfamiliar front porch. I gently laid a note and a bag of opened and carefully re-closed apples onto a comfy sitting chair. I made friends with a big, old dog that was running free. My work was done and I was gone.

    I had forgotten about the events of the early morning by the time the phone call came. There was unintelligible screaming and sobbing in my ear for a moment or two. Then I realized that it was just a woman who had prayed a prayer of desperation and gotten an answer from the Lord! She didn't give me many details. I didn't ask for them, nor did I need them. I only know that she too, was needing to hear something specific at a particular moment in time and God met her!

    Thinking about God's love for me and for others was an amazing thing. My faith began to increase. I started telling the apple story whenever the opportunity arose. I remember writing a letter, baking a special apple cobbler, and taking it to Monroe, the neighbor who gave me the apples from the Lord.

*He's going to know I'm crazy. He's going to think I'm nuts. He might even worry that I've gone insane, but he's going to hear that God used him to make a difference in my life!*

    When we drove down the hill to his house on Thanksgiving morning, I was scared and full of peace all at the same time. Greg offered to take the cobbler and the letter to the front door and explain the story. Before long, out of the house came Greg, Monroe, and his wife. They came over and met our children and wished us a happy Thanksgiving. They talked about the importance of kindness, offered us some turnips and walnuts, and rejoiced with us in the faithfulness of our Lord!

**Lord,**
    **Thank you for Monroe. Thank you for using him to help answer my prayer. Lord, I pray that You would bless him and his entire family for their faithfulness to You. I pray that You would meet their needs and draw very near to them.**
    **I'm so thankful Lord that Monroe was obedient to You, that he was in the right place, at the right time, to be used. I pray that You will keep using him and his family. I pray that he will know how very vital he is in Your work and Your kingdom!**

# A Season of Intimacy

## Chapter Four

  Thinking about God's love for me increased my faith. If God heard my prayer for apples, He must hear every other prayer I pray. He must take the time to listen to the concerns of my heart. I knew I had a privilege and a responsibility to take my prayer life more seriously. There were many hurting people in the world who needed God's love in their lives. They needed to know that God could hear them. He could heal them. He could change them and make them more like Him, if they only believed in Him. I began to pray with faith.
  One of the first things I asked God for, with faith, was personal healing. As I mentioned before, I had been suffering from migraine cluster headaches for quite some time. I had tried several medical treatments to no avail. Even the expensive pain medications only helped for a few hours. I couldn't justify spending money on pain medicine when it barely even helped me. Many people suffer from headaches, for a variety of reasons. My headaches, I was told, were caused by some kind of neurological problem that started

after I had a complicated surgery to remove a tumor on my adrenal gland, caused by a rare endocrine disease. Along with the headaches, I experienced occasional loss of balance and some short-term memory loss.

Shortly after I started praying with faith and opening myself up to be prayed for by others who prayed with faith, I received an answer to prayer that was both wonderful and surprising. My neurologist put me on an inexpensive medication that really helped my pain. It was the first time in nearly a year that I was without a headache for an entire weekend. I was thrilled. Then I started noticing some side effects.

First of all, everything I ate tasted sort of bitter. I could stand to lose a few pounds, so that was fine. Next, it made me sleepy. That was harder to deal with, because I lead a very active life. However, after many months of pain, I figured I'd rather be a bit dopey than always hurting. Sometimes I would doubt whether this was the Lord's help for me or not. I knew God had the power to completely heal me and take my headaches away. I also knew that I was finally out of pain. I could shake my head, stand in a bright room, and even drive with the radio up loud! The headaches were gone. I felt very peaceful about this medication being a gift from the Lord, but then again, maybe I was just sleepy!

The worst side effect, however, was the memory loss. The medicine exacerbated a problem I already struggled with. I gave the medicine a good, old college try. I worked with it, taught with it, and even tried to memorize a song or two with it. However, the medicine made my memory issues so unbearable that I couldn't even memorize my song for the

Christmas program. It was getting increasingly difficult to cope. I remember praying one morning before church:

**Lord,**

**Was this my miracle? I wanted to be out of pain and healed Lord! This is out of pain and stupid. I forgot where I parked last week, Lord. I feel like everywhere I go, everything I do, every breath I take, every little move I make, I need Your help. I feel like I depend on You for everything. Some people need You for their water and air and food and clothes. Lord, I need You for life, for sustenance. It's like I can't breathe on my own. My heart can't beat on its own. I can't eat for myself or drink for myself. You have to feed me with an umbilical chord, Lord. I am so dependent on You. I want to be ...**

Before I could finish my prayer, I realized what I was saying. Did I really want to be free? Free from God? I needed God and was complaining about it. I relied so much on Him those days to find things, to understand basic things, to remember things I had known just a few hours before. God always came through for me.

**Lord,**
**I'm sorry. I'm so glad that You've been here for me. I'm so glad that I need You as I do. I want to depend on You. I want to rely on You for every breath, every heartbeat, every thought, and every deed. I want You to know how much I need you and long for You Lord. If it weren't for You Lord, I wouldn't be able to make it in this world. You, in me, makes my life possible. I'm so glad I have You Lord. I'm so glad I need You Lord. You're my best friend!**

I began to realize that though the medication slowed my mind down, it also slowed me down. I started noticing that I could hear God's voice louder and clearer. I started hearing him speak to me all the time. I began developing an intimate relationship with the Lord.

One Saturday afternoon, the children were all visiting at Grandma's and Grandpa's house. Greg was out working in his shop and I had finished some chores inside the house. I sat in my favorite comfortable spot with a perfect view outside. I began looking up to the sky and talking to God. I don't remember what I was saying or what God was saying to me, but I was lost in His presence. Then Greg walked in.

"What ya doin'?" he asked as he went into the kitchen, washed his hands, and poured a glass of water.

"Just ...praying," I quietly answered, trying hard not to sound annoyed or frustrated.

"Oh," he responded back quickly. "Carry on." He left

almost as quickly as he came in.

When I was alone with God again, I was filled with joy at a new realization. I wanted to be alone with God. I wanted quality time with Him, uninterrupted, just Him and I. I was bothered when my husband interrupted my time with my Savior!

Greg and I had often looked at each other in that knowing way when a child interrupted our conversation. We had often 'tried hard' not to show our annoyance as our children infringed upon 'our time' together. This was the first time I had ever experienced that feeling with God. My prayer time had been interrupted before, but this time, God and I were having an intimate conversation.

It was 'our time,' and hard to accept an intrusion.

*A passionate longing for GOD will surely never disappoint, for it shall be filled.*

## Chapter Five

The only thing better than growing in the Lord, is growing in the Lord at Christmas time! I love Christmas. I love the traditional smells and sights and sounds. I love to deck the halls, the kitchen, the bathroom, and any other space I can find. I love to blast the Christmas music and have something yummy in the oven just in case guests show up unexpectedly. I love teaching our children how to give and I really love teaching our children that Christmas is only so special because it's all about Jesus.

With all that said, this Christmas was really all about Jesus! Due to a combination of health bills and a rental property that was losing money, this year's Christmas budget was thin. Greg and I decided that we would exchange cards with each other so that we could give more to our children, family, and friends. We were already so very blessed and it gave us great joy to be able to focus on the needs of others.

We usually go to our favorite Christmas tree farm the

weekend after Thanksgiving, but this year our financial situation had delayed our expedition. One might think our spirits would have been down, but it was actually quite the opposite. You see, God took amazing care of us during that time. As soon as I mentioned needing something to God, it seemed to show up.

*Sometimes when we pray, we say "amen." We say it to signify that we are in agreement with the words we have just spoken. More often though, I believe we say, "amen" to conclude a prayer. If prayer is simply communication with God, then why conclude at all? I decided that there would be 'no more amens' in my life. That is, I did not want to say goodbye to Jesus.*

*Now, instead of a morning prayer, mealtime grace, and occasional requests made throughout the day, I can talk to God all day long. I don't have to start with the traditional "Dear Lord, I'm here again, because I never left Him. Working, driving, and even grocery shopping are much more enjoyable with the Lord by my side. I realize that there is value in 'amen' in corporate settings, but personally, I've banned the word from my vocabulary.*

We wanted to buy some gifts for a few families that we knew were going through some hard times. We prayed. All of a sudden, an unexpected end-of-the-year check showed up from work. That kind of "bonus" had never come before, nor has it come since.

I started wanting a Christmas tree and kindly asked

the Lord to provide. My dad showed up and said, "I noticed you haven't gotten your tree yet, I hope it's okay. if..."

"Of course it's okay. Thanks Dad! I want you know you were used by God in an answer to my prayers!"

It was our first ever lot-bought Christmas tree! It was like unwrapping an early Christmas present. We had no idea what it looked like until it was all put up in the stand! When it was all decorated, it turned out to be one of our all-time favorite trees!

**Lord,**
**You are so thoughtful to me! You keep giving and giving and giving to me and my family. I'm amazed at Your generosity Lord. I want You to know that all I really want for Christmas is YOU!**

God kept giving and giving. I kept telling Him my needs and desires, but emphasizing that He was what I really wanted. I wrote a song called, "All I want for Christmas is You." I sang it to the Lord throughout the whole Christmas season. Jesus drew nearer and nearer, or maybe it was me stepping toward Him. In any case, blessings poured in from near and far away.

There were special aunts and uncles who blessed us with gifts and money. They have always been such instruments of the Lord in our life. There were Grandmas and Grandpas who shared blessings of many kinds. We'll never forget their generous support and loving kindness. There was also our wonderful church family who surprised us with an amazing showering of gifts for our entire family. They have always been a steadfast beacon of unconditional love and encouragement.

**Lord,**
**I said all I wanted was <u>You</u>. Why are You pouring out more blessings than I ever asked for or even dreamed of? I don't understand Lord. I really don't get it. This is <u>too much</u>!**

*Sometimes when God blesses you over and over and over again, you can start feeling guilty and unworthy for being the recipient of so many blessings. You can actually start turning away blessings, believing the enemy's lies that you are 'hoarding the goodness of God.' During those times, it is ever-increasingly important to know the truth. You are a child of God. He loves you immensely, cares for you deeply, and finds great joy in blessing all His children. The vital truth is that the bounty of the Lord has no limitations nor knows any end.*

# Lord, help me see. It's not about me.

Whenever I started believing the lies of the enemy, the Voice of Truth would draw me closer, convincing me otherwise. I began to walk with my head held higher, with my heart loving my King deeper. I knew the truth: it had nothing to do with me and everything to do with Him!

Greg and I had been praying fervently for our finances. We had prayed for months that all of our medical bills could be paid by the end of the year. God performed amazing miracles right in front of our eyes. We ended the year with the last bill paid!

## Chapter Six

*Having an intimate relationship with God is an awesome thing. I learned how to live in a brand new way. My greatest fear was somehow losing this longing for God, this special connection I felt with my Savior.*

  My headaches had basically disappeared by the Spring of 2005. I was used to my new pain-free life! The side effects from my medication were becoming increasingly troublesome though. After praying a great deal, I approached my doctor about lowering my medication. To my joy, my doctor came up with a new medication plan that lessened my side effects a great deal!
  I could now take less of the medication that made me so tired and forgetful and take it at night! I didn't mind being tired or dopey when I was sleeping!
  I was frightened though. If my mind sped up, would I still be able to hear God? Would I feel His leading me to pray as I had before? Would I get 'busy' again and be easily

distracted and detracted? It was time to face my fears.

I purposed in my mind that I was going to stay close to the Lord. If I never left His side, we couldn't grow apart. I discovered that God didn't leave with the change of my medication. I was relieved and so thankful. Then I had a moment of panic.

About half way through an especially busy day, I noticed that God hadn't spoken to me all day. That is, I hadn't felt strongly prompted to pray for anyone in particular or to help anyone in any out-of-the-ordinary way. I felt awkward and different, as if God were ignoring me. I immediately confronted Him.

**Lord,**

**Are You mad at me? I'm trying to figure out what I've done wrong today. I want to be used by You. Please Lord, don't take Your presence from me. I beg You Lord. Just let me know what I need to do to hear from You again and I'll do it. I love talking with You and praying for people and feeling You ask me to intercede for people Lord. I longed for You for so long Lord. I'm crying out to You, don't let things change, Lord. I'm sorry if I've done something wrong Lord. Show me what it is and I'll change it. I just want to be close to You again. I'll wait right here until I feel You again, Lord. I'm not going anywhere. I'm desperate for You in my life.**

I waited for the Lord. I was prepared to wait as long as He took. A short time later, I felt God's presence with me strongly again. He hadn't left me. He was close by. We just had a busy day and I couldn't see Him or feel Him for a short time.

I learned some very valuable things that day. Sometimes I feel God and sometimes I don't. During the times when schedules are hectic and activities are looming, God doesn't leave. He is close by. I abide in Christ, but when I look into the eyes of the hurting, my focus is temporarily shared. After a day of giving and serving in many avenues, I need to be careful that my focus is on Jesus. He is the one who fills me up so I can pour myself out again. I also learned that God desires for this 'season of intimacy' to last forever. It's a journey toward Him that is never supposed to end. I found great comfort in that realization.

**Thank You Lord,**

**For the realization You have given Me. You never leave! I get busy and my focus wanders sometimes, but you always want a relationship with me. You are a gracious, merciful God. I love You so dearly, Lord. Thank You for giving Your wisdom, for speaking to me specifically. Thank You for being right by my side.**

During this season of intimacy with my Heavenly Father, I felt I could do anything. I was starting to realize that if God was right beside me, I could fly if He wanted me to. As I grew closer to the Lord, I also felt Him ask more of me. The things He asked me to do no longer seemed impossible. Though fear and doubt still reared their ugly heads at times, my Abba Father quickly chased them away.

In the late Spring of 2005, the Lord began speaking to Greg and I about adopting again. In fact, God spoke quite poignantly to our whole family. Specifically, He wanted us to adopt twin 10 year olds.

We had been down the adoption road before with our first three children, but when we adopted them, they were 6 months, 3 years, and 4 years old. Adopting older children would be a new experience.

The Lord is all-knowing and all-powerful. He has our best interest at heart. He sees the whole picture of our lives, while we see just what He allows. We knew and recognized the awesomeness of our God, but we proceeded with fear in our hearts. Sometimes obeying the Lord isn't easy. Complete trust and faith in Him are imperative. However, we must obey. Our twins needed a family that knew about stubborn love and unconditional acceptance. We felt God was saying they needed us. Our busy family of five became a bigger family of seven.

*I'd love to write another book, another day about adopting older children. For now though, let me just share that God has given us such amazing treasures in our children. We have started each of our adoption journeys thinking solely that we were reaching out to the children. A few steps into each journey, however, we discovered that the joy and blessing was indeed ours. We are so very thankful that our fear and apprehension didn't stop us from claiming the treasures of the Lord.*

**Thank you Lord,**
**For entrusting two more precious children to us. Thank you for asking us to be their parents. Thank you for drawing near to us so that we could hear your voice clearly and trust your heart. Just months ago, I'm sure we would have run from You. We would have let fear rule our decisions. Thank You for building our faith and for building our family. Thank You for loving us so much that You draw near to us. We are so very blessed.**

# A Season Of Striving

## Chapter Seven

I grew up the eldest of two daughters. We both worked hard to make our parents proud from the very beginning of our lives. We were taught to keep our bedrooms tidy, to complete our household chores, and to work hard in school. I don't ever remember turning in a half-hearted school project. The thought never crossed my mind. I knew that school was my 'job,' and I needed to do my very best.

I remember writing and directing and 'starring' in my own musicals as a young girl and inviting the entire neighborhood over to see them. I could usually talk my sister, Amy, into playing several difficult roles. She had an excellent memory, was a talented performer, and loved the spotlight as much as I did! Sometimes we'd do two-three shows a year, depending on whether my parents were feeling especially generous about having 10-12 kids run around their house for several days for "rehearsals." Often, my best friend, Kim, would join us too. We'd tell the neighborhood about Jesus and we always had a good turnout!

I think I was about fourteen the first time my mother took me aside and talked to me about what drove me, about why I did what I did. It was good for me to hear myself say aloud, that I was 'motivated by what others thought about me.' I wanted others to like me, so I tried as hard as I could to be perfect. Perfection was an unrealistic goal, of course, so I grew increasingly discouraged with myself.

I remember my mother saying, "Let's concentrate on the things you can and should change, rather than the things you cannot or shouldn't change." Mom and I made a list and suddenly life seemed easier. I needed to change my focus. I needed to stop striving.

I have been "striving" since the day I was born. Part of it is probably genetic or generational. I come from a family of strivers. It seems we are always trying to do more, be more, give more, and learn more. It's hard not to let this get out of balance in my life though, especially in my walk with the Lord.

Striving is not a new season for me. It's been a season that has come and gone many times in my life. I remember some time ago hearing the Lord tell me something very strange. I thought He told me to put my Bible away for a while. The very thought of putting my Bible away…surely that can't be from the Lord. Then my mind and heart were flooded with thoughts of striving and earning and trying to be better than I currently was. In some way, I believed that if I exerted enough energy and will, then I would somehow be able to acquire more of God's love or approval. In short, I thought if I read enough, understood enough, and memorized enough of God's Word that I would prove something to Him.

I was striving to do the work that God wanted to do in me. I put my Bible away.

I quickly discovered that I 'wanted' to read my Bible, that I actually longed to read it. I believe that God wanted to show me that I could read for a whole new reason. I didn't need to read to prove anything to Him. He knows me better than I know myself. I didn't need to read to earn His love either. For He loved me while I was still a sinner, and He never changes. I could read simply to learn about my God, to let Him speak to me in another way, to draw nearer to Him. I read again, because I longed for more of God.

Reading my Bible became a new experience for me. I began to find passages and meditate on them, sometimes just reading one chapter or set of verses over and over for several weeks. I was really learning the lessons and principles in that passage. God was speaking to me in a brand new way.

John 15 was an especially special passage to me. I loved the analogy of Christ being the Vine and God being the Gardener. As I meditated on this section of scripture, I started seeing myself as a branch. Whenever I began to struggle, I knew that I needed to rely on the Lord more. I was grafted into Him at the moment I gave Him my heart, but my sinful nature desired to sever my attachment to the Vine. I was striving to do more and be more in order to grow more fruit. The Lord showed me that He wanted to bear my fruit through me. Being a branch, I desperately needed to stay attached to Him, the Vine. He was the source of any fruit I would ever bear.

It's amazing to me, to this day, that I didn't see him coming. I didn't see the enemy creeping in with his clever lies. He hit so subtly that only in hindsight can I see that he was hiding in my insecurities. At some point, my greatest fear turned from '*somehow losing my longing for God,*' to somehow disappointing the people who were counting on me.

*The music was the first thing to go. It was such a gradual, easing into busy-ness and activity that I didn't even notice at first. I had been singing and writing songs since I was a little girl, so I should have noticed when the music began to fade. Spontaneous songs of praise and personal expression to my Lord became a struggle. Then I began to sing out of habit, rather than relationship. It all happened so dreadfully slowly, so slow it sometimes appeared to be my active imagination. The joy and light in my eyes turned into drive and determination. I found myself needing to succeed and achieve in order to feel accepted by God. I felt that He had given me certain responsibilities and expected me to triumph. My focus, ever so slightly, turned from Him………… to myself.*

*I never would have described myself as a 'selfish' person. After all, I focused most of my energy on serving others and their needs. However, my self loathing and engrossment in my limitations took on a personality all of their own. I wasn't focused on meeting my own needs, like in the sense we usually think of in the term selfishness. I was focused on my insecurities. Nevertheless, I was focused on me and my selfishness could not be helpful or healthy.*

# Chapter 8

Five children outnumber 2 parents. Five children eat a lot and go through a lot of laundry. Five children make for some sleepless nights and exhausting days. I longed to be a wonderful mother and an attentive wife. I also desired to be a loyal employee, an inspiring Sunday School teacher, and an excellent parent volunteer in each of my children's classrooms. In my efforts to be my best, my priorities became misaligned.

I spent many months trying to be good enough. 'Good enough' never replaced the feelings of doubt and guilt that I carried when I couldn't do all I wanted. 'Good enough' never encouraged me or held me in the dark moments. 'Good enough' never came. I kept striving, somehow believing, that a little more attention to detail and a little less sleep would help me meet my goals. Eventually, I hit a rock solid wall. This wall was constructed of high ideals, perfectionistic tendencies, and unrealistic expectations. My world seemed to be caving in around me and I insisted on striving more in order to push to the other side. All the while, I tried to keep any onlookers fooled. 'I could do it all if I just exerted enough energy.' There would be a price to pay for my independence.

*Why do we keep doing the same old things when we should know that they'll never work? Why do we push ourselves harder and harder only to learn that what we are striving for has already been given to us, free of charge, free of worry, free of work? The Lord accepts us just as we are. Why do we keep trying to prove our worth to Him, to earn His love?*

My season of striving led me to a place where I honestly thought I'd never be. It led me to the depths of despair and to a land of independence. I never thought I'd ever want to be independent again. I knew that I needed God for my very breath. I asked myself what I was doing here. Yet, deep inside, I knew how I'd come to this treacherous place.

In the midst of all my striving, I found myself desperate to succeed at everything. I found myself discouraged with my rate of progress. I found myself trying harder, sleeping less, and eventually deciding that I *couldn't* do it all. This realization was terrifying to me, for I felt that everything I was involved in was not only important and worthwhile, but also my God-given responsibilities. It was crucial that I did not fail. I figured that this busy time in my life would be short-lived. I just needed a little reprieve from somewhere in order to get a little more time to strive. I made a calculated, coherent decision that I soon came to regret.

**Lord,**

**It seems like the evil one is looming around me, just watching for me to fail. It seems as if I will never get caught up at work, at home, in ministry and my relationships. I feel like I'm falling apart Lord. Something has to give. Work is so busy and they need me to hang in there. My family is struggling and I need to make sure I meet their needs. People all over are hurting Lord. I can't turn them away. I need to show them who You are. God, you are the only one who sees all of this. I'm exhausted. If I don't get some sleep, sickness and weariness is going to overtake me. I know You get it Lord. You will be there tomorrow or later in the week. You won't leave me if I don't spend time with You. The rest of the world doesn't understand. I'm sorry Lord that You are the one I'm placing on hold, but You are the only one who gets this life I'm living. I love You, Lord. Thank you for understanding.**

I honestly thought about what I was saying to the Lord before I said it. The fact that I knew what I was saying is as scary to me as what I said. I told the Lord that I couldn't spend time with Him because I was too busy. I told the Lord that I thought He'd be sympathetic with my dilemma; after all it was His work I was trying to do, His important work. Essentially, I was telling God I didn't need Him. I was going spiritually blind.

When I look back to this time in my life, I am ashamed, filled with regret, and deeply sorry. I was completely blinded by my striving. I chose to walk away from the Lord, knowing that I would come back later. What I didn't realize, is how hard and long the road back would be. I know now what a terrible decision I made, but at that time, it seemed like the only logical choice.

## *Who Am I?*

*Who am I Lord to think that I could ever*
*Ever even make my heart beat on its own?*

*Who am I Lord? I've never parted waters*
*never freed my children, or led them to their home*

*Who am I Lord to feel that I could counsel,*
*Counsel my Dear Maker on what He should do?*

*Who am I Lord? I haven't healed a blind man,*
*Haven't raised a dead man,*
*I've just believed in You.*

    I regretted my decision almost immediately, realizing what I had done. I desperately needed the Lord, yet I had told Him to wait. Guilt and shame welled up inside of me and I started dropping some of the balls I was juggling. I was becoming ineffective in my ministry, easily frustrated with my family, and overloaded at work.

When I was a young teenager, facing typical teen heartaches and pressures, my wise mother took me aside and shared a piece of valuable wisdom. She had noticed that I was carrying burdens that I had no business lugging around on my own. These were hurts and worries that were much too heavy, never meant for me to carry alone. She told me that I needed to share the burdens with her. She said that God had placed her in my life for many reasons, but one of them was to share in my trials. She likened my life to a jellybean jar and my burdens were like the pieces of candy that filled the jar! Each piece was so important to me that I didn't want to share it. The jar could only hold so many pieces though, so unless I wanted an explosion, I needed to choose to share. I simply could not consume all of those jellybeans. When it was explained to me so simply, I began to understand. I began to see that sharing my burdens is not hurting others, but in fact trusting them and blessing them with more of me. I was only made to contain so much, so I need to let go of what I cannot hold.

*Sharing a burden can strengthen a friendship.*

As an adult and a child of God, I should have known better. However, I tried very hard to hide my struggles from those I know now would have loved to help me. I believed that asking for or even accepting help that was offered was somehow admitting that I was a failure and couldn't do it myself. No one seemed to notice my collapsing. I had successfully managed to fool those around me. I could literally feel my joy leaving me. Everything I did was a chore, a drudgery. My striving reached an all-time high and my confidence reached an all-time low. My songs of praise to the Lord became songs of despair. Then I stopped singing altogether. The jellybean jar that was me, was bursting. I needed to be completely rebuilt.

**Lord,
I don't know where to start. Help me. Please. Help me, before I completely die Lord. I can't do anything anymore. I'm so sorry, so sorry. Please help me.**

The Lord never whispered, 'I told you so,' or 'it's about time you ungrateful child.' He just listened to me, stayed with me, and told me to rest. I tried to rest, but it seemed to be easier said than done. I asked the Lord to help me see how I could do all He was asking.

He led me to the following scriptures:

Matthew 11:28-30 *"Come to Me all you who labor and are heavy laden, and I will give you rest. Take My yoke upon you and learn from Me, for I am gentle and lowly in heart, and you will find rest for your souls. For My yoke is easy and My burden is light."*

Isaiah 30:15 *"This is what the Sovereign LORD, the Holy One of Israel, says: "In repentance and rest is your salvation, in quietness and trust is your strength..."*

God began to speak to me as I took the time to be still before Him and rest in His presence. The rest I experienced was an inward rest in which my spirit was renewed. Taking on the Lord's yoke meant taking off the weight of the world. Christ was a gentle leader who humbled Himself in order to serve me. His easy burden felt more like an extension of myself than my burden ever could.

This time of recovery took several months and my growth was slow. It was extremely difficult for me to trade in my yoke and accept the yoke of the Lord and the rest that came with it. Some days I would take two steps forward. Other days I would fall three steps behind. Striving had become a disease in me that only resting in the Lord could cure. I had to force myself to believe the truth rather than the lies I had told myself and let the enemy fool me into believing. To this day, the Lord is still rebuilding me after my time of self-destruction.

# Chapter Nine

In recalling this dark season of my life, I realize that striving had become a diseased way of life for me. During my rebuilding, I needed to let the Lord speak the truth to me. God began to reset my priorities and change my focus. Instead of doing and being, I was taught to listen, to trust, and to rest. I wasn't always a good student of the Lord, but I kept trying. Slow progress led to lasting change.

I made a commitment to myself and to the Lord that I would never be independent again. The destruction I had felt inside as a result of my independence was more than I could bear. As I started taking more steps toward the Lord, I began to realize just how fragile and vulnerable I was. I knew that I had the power to let myself become independent again. I was not immune to making the same mistake a second time....and a third time for that matter. I concentrated on living in the present, but I also frequently visited the past.

In Joshua 4, it speaks about stones of remembrance. These stones were set in place by the Israelites to remind them of the faithfulness of God. I never wanted to visit this spiritual desolation again and set to setting up various stones of remembrance for myself. I wrote songs about the mercy and compassion of the Lord, poems about God's power and loving forgiveness, and I journalled about the entire journey away from and back to God.

*Journalling is an excellent way to leave the past in the past, yet have it available for a reminder when it's needed. I have journalled off and on throughout my life and love looking back to my youth, and my growth throughout the years. When I look back to the journals of this season of striving in my life, I see such hopelessness and despair. Reading my own words and thoughts of this time helps me to purpose that I must never be independent again.*

*On my journey back to the Lord, my journal was filled with initial prayers of repentance and regret. The first song I wrote during my recovery called out to God in desperation. I hated the darkness around me. I longed to be connected to the Vine once more.*

# Lord, I am repenting. It's all that I can do.

## Withered Grape

Sitting here, On my bed,
Staring at the wall,
Can barely begin to start a prayer,
With the Creator of it all.

I'm so dried up, so decayed
That I've begun to stink.
There's no sign of life in here.
I'm too far gone, I think.

How did I get to this decrepit place?
How come I've lost the focus on Your face?
Where oh where, Lord, is Your sweet embrace?
I cannot feel Your gentleness and grace.

I've never been to where I am right now.
All I can do is sit and wonder how.
How did I let this awful dying come?
When did I turn my back from my home?

Is there any going back?
Is it too late for me?
Am I too dead and dying
To live again with Thee?

Lord help me. Lord, help me.
I'm calling out to You.
Lord, I am repenting.
It's all that I can do.

As I cried out to God, I learned to listen again, instead of always lamenting to or asking from Him. Once again, God began speaking to me. He gave me dreams to think about and set a new focused purpose on my life. I was eager to spend time with Him again, and His blessing and joy returned to me. Though I knew I had been restored and forgiven, I remained constantly aware that I had the power to destroy myself once, and I never wanted to walk down that road again. It was on a family camping trip, out in the woods that I love, that I finally made the dogged decision that my striving needed to end forever.

*Initially, I thought it was something I could control and just monitor closely. I soon realized that I couldn't control my own striving any better than an addict can control the amount of substance he abuses. Striving was bigger than me. It still is. Only God, in me, can conquer it. "I can do all things through Christ who strengthens me." (Philippians 4:13)*

I turned over my striving and began to really rest in the Lord. Music filled my heart again and I longed to sing before the Lord. I desperately wanted to see all that I had been missing.

### I Haven't Seen the Stars

*I know I've been runnin' for quite some time.*
*And often I've been worried I'm just fallin' more behind.*
*My life's gotten crazy.   I'm all mixed up inside.*
*Lord I'm realizin'   perhaps that I've been blind.*

*I haven't seen the stars in quite a long, long time.*
*I haven't watched the sun go down  or met it at its rise.*
*I haven't chased a rainbow in I don't know how long.*
*I haven't stopped to smell a rose or sing a campfire song.*
*I haven't seen the stars.*

*When I try to slow down, demands are made on me.*
*I know I've got to hurry to be all that I can be.*
*But with all this movin,'    I'm not reachin' my goal.*
*And all this hustle bustle  is takin' it's toll.*
*I haven't seen the stars in quite a long, long time.*
*I haven't watched the sun go down or met it at its rise.*
*I  haven't chased a rainbow   in I don't know how long.*
*I haven't stopped to smell a rose or sing a campfire song.*
*I haven't seen the stars.*

*Lord I don't know how to slow this ship down.*
*I don't know how to turn this life around.*
*It's getting clearer every moment…   I've been in control,*
*and I'm finally ready Lord to let it go.*

*Because I haven't seen the stars in the longest time.*
*I know this is not Your plan  for this life of mine.*
*You have much much more for me, if I let it go.*
*So here Lord, take control.*
*I want to see the stars.*

*I want to see the stars!  I want to watch them shine.*
*I want to search the sky and see what I can find*
*and smile at the moon and dream that I can fly!*
*Oh, I want to see the stars!*

I longed to hear the voice of the Lord as I had during the season when I had known Him intimately. I knew that God desired to have a close relationship with me too. He wanted me to be a sheep who recognized my Master's familiar tone.

*I have a good friend who lived on a farm and cared for sheep during her college years. She talks about those sheep with smiled fondness. Apparently, sheep aren't the most intelligent creatures in the pasture! In fact, Pastor Taunja describes them as downright dumb at times! We are called the Lord's sheep and He is our Shepherd! We need the Lord! Without Him, we'd be lost, cold, wet, and starving. The Shepherd wants us to depend on Him and listen for His voice.*

I must have gently spoken to Greg a dozen times about quitting my job and home schooling our children. Each time he responded with the same fears and doubts that I initially had. We couldn't afford to live on one income. Educating five children would be quite an undertaking for someone who studied social work, rather than education. Maybe God was just calling us to slow our lives down a bit, not drastically change them.

After several months, Greg and I agreed to ask the Lord to speak to us together, confirming whether or not He was telling us to make this huge change in our lives. After all, we both agreed wholeheartedly that if God was speaking to one of us, He would confirm what He was saying to both of us. It is never God's desire to confuse or bring disunity into a marriage. God spoke and confirmed very clearly to both of us. We were to trust in Him and obey. We were to step out of the boat, onto the water, trusting in the Lord. The real adventure began!

As we obeyed, the Lord showed both of us just how easy His yolk was. We found His burden to be so very light. The Lord took our strivings and showed us just how futile they were. He took our burdens and replaced them with His ways. Our joy grew and our heaviness of heart melted away.

*Our own nature said, 'you can't do it.' God said, 'I can.' Our own nature believed that we could not afford it. God knew He would take care of every need we had. Our own nature argued, 'what will people think? We can't let them down. They expect us to...' God said, 'I am the one you should desire to please. I know you better than anyone else does. Obey Me.' Our own nature felt that it was impossible. The God of the Universe showed us His power!*

Working hard and doing our best should be important to all Christians. In our efforts to be and do, however, we often lose our focus. We can stray from seeing ourselves as God sees us, and start focusing on our failures. When our focus turns from the Lord, we can start striving in our own strength.

Striving can be deadly. It can lead to independence and self-destruction. Striving can be debilitating and it is a robber of joy, peace, and faith. Striving is natural for us. We long to do well, to be successful, and to show that we have earned and even deserve a pat on the back.

Jesus paid for each of us. He chose to give His life to end our striving for acceptance and redemption. God chose to unconditionally love us. All we need to do is accept His gift.

**My Dear Child,**
   **I've missed you today! Even though we've been together the whole day through, it's not the same as it is right now, when it's just you and Me. I love the way you look up into the sky, wherever you are, looking for Me! I notice and I'm right there. I love the way your eyes sparkle when someone says My name or mentions something wonderful I've done. I especially love the way you rearrange your entire day just so you and I can have some quiet time together. I love you, you know. I love you with My life. I love you from the top of your tired head to the bottom of your aching feet. I notice that you get up early to get all of the things done that you need to do. I notice when you stay up late to say goodnight to Me after the last crumb is swept up off the floor. I love that you love your family and I love that you love Me more. I know you are trying to change the things about yourself that aren't pleasing to Me. Remember though that I want to help you. I don't even want you to try to do it on your own. It makes you weary. It wears you out. Only I have the strength to do such things. I can and will if you'll just let**

*Me. I love that you need Me as you do. I smile at the thought of helping you. You are strong and capable, My child. I created you that way. All my children need me though and I am glad that you are recognizing that more and more. I long to help you, you know. I long to hold you, to strengthen you, and encourage you all along the way. I want to do this for all My children – So remember as you try to look to my other children for encouragement – that they are on a parallel path to yours and Mine. They too need to look to Me for their strength and support. You cannot save them. I must. My Child, you are special to Me. I see you every second of every day. There is only one you. I know everything about you, that you were tired this morning, that you were lonely last night. I saw you when you almost cried a little earlier today. I'm here with you now. Don't let there be any distractions, or any other people, just you and Me. Pour out your heart to Me. I'm listening. Tell Me your hopes and dreams, and even your fears. Tell me all of it. Then listen closely as I tell you my plans for you.*

      *Love,*
    *Your Heavenly Father*

*Striving brings work and worry. Leaning on the Lord brings peace and joy!*

# A Season of Dreaming

# Chapter 10

I have discovered blindness in my life many times. I have finally concluded that even what I thought was perfect sight, is only slightly better sight than what I learned to be blindness earlier. Tomorrow or soon after my eyes will see yet more clearly and I will learn how truly blind I am today. This is the journey I am on.

*Several years ago, when I was a student in college, I started experiencing some problems with my equilibrium. I noticed that when I was standing up with my eyes closed, I needed to hold onto something, or I'd feel as if I might fall. Nausea was also common during those episodes. Times of corporate worship were especially difficult for me, as I loved to stand, close my eyes, and raise my hands to the Lord. Out of necessity, I developed a habit of worshiping with my eyes open.*

*It was only recently that I noticed that I no longer experienced dizziness or nausea as I worshiped my Lord with closed eyes. I felt the Lord's still, small voice say to me, "you have done well worshiping with open eyes. Now you must learn how worship Me with closed eyes. You must worship when you can't see Me clearly or when you don't know where I am or what I am doing. You need to trust Me recklessly and worship Me in your blindness."*

At one time, I thought I saw so clearly, as I ran from place to place trying to care for all that God placed in front of me. Now, I realize that I saw only what I was looking at, what the world had presented to me as the truth. I was blinded by what I was seeing. *"Now we see things imperfectly as in a cloudy mirror, but then we will see everything with perfect clarity."* (NLT) 1 Corinthians 13:12

As our eyes continue to become more opened to the Lord, God has shown us that He has plans that are not only way beyond what we can imagine, but are also superior to anything we believe to be wise or knowledgeable. The Lord's ways are simply higher than our ways. We fail to see His wisdom sometimes because it is so contrary to what the world says, and there's so much of the world in us.

*The world says, 'save and keep your money.' God says, 'give it away. I will repay you many times over.' The world says, 'work harder, strive more, and maybe you can get ahead.' God says, trust in Me, obey Me, and I will see that you thrive.' The world says 'live for yourself,' and 'look out for number one.'  God says, 'you will gain life when you give life away.'*

    We had (and have) a lot to learn, but we've sure been amazed as we've done it!  We caught a glimpse of the vastness of God.  Chapter upon chapter could be written explaining the miracles that have taken place since we've stepped out of the boat.  God has turned around our faith.  He's taken complete control over our finances.  He's steering our future.  We can finally declare that the Lord is at the wheel.  We couldn't do this when we were living according to the world's wisdom, using our human sight.  We had to live by faith.
    Seeing the Lord at work has given us hope for the future.  Seeing His provision helps us to keep the focus off of our limitations and onto His will and might.  Dreams that Greg and I were previously afraid to mention aloud are now being talked about and prayed over daily.  We've begun to believe that God can do anything.  After all, He can!


*"For I know the thoughts that I think toward you," says the Lord, "thoughts of peace and not of evil, to give you a future and a hope."*     Jeremiah 29:11

Lord,
when we can't see You or even hear You, help us to be still in just knowing You and that You always have our best at heart.

# Chapter 11

When you have a driving, God-given dream, you think about it a lot. I'll never forget the first vision I had regarding our dream. The Lord showed me the lay of the land. I watched with deep anticipation as He showed me various rooms and buildings on the property that would one day be our camp.

It started with something like a virtual tour of the log-lodge home. The home was at the center of the family, like the heart of the camp. So many meaningful exchanges and experiences took place in the home. The home I saw was more than an image, it was an intense expression. There was such an amazing unity of purpose there. Each family member knew their value and significance, and each flowed beautifully in their roles. I sensed that the family was much larger than just the seven of us.

As I stepped onto the large wrap-around porch, toward the open door, more of the scene unfolded. I walked into the massive front room and looked up at the vaulted ceilings and loft overlooking this great room. I instinctually knew that the bedrooms were up the stairs in the loft above. Off of the front room were two other large rooms. One was a place of learning, with globes, books, tables, and a large window encompassing the entire back wall. Up close to the ceiling was a shelf that wrapped around the perimeter of the room. On this shelf, were the years of rocks, fossils, and shells that our family had gathered. The other room was a large family room with a brown-leathered sectional sofa, large comfortable pillows, and throws. There was a square pine coffee table loaded messily with magazines and books. On the sides of a large old television was a tall, wide built-in cabinet with games and puzzles loaded on the exposed shelves. In the back of the room, was a long, picnic-like table perfect for projects. I could see a half-finished puzzle lying unattended next to a waiting game of Monopoly. The entire scene overlooked another windowed back wall. There was a small patio just outside.

I also saw a small room off the great front room that appeared to be a den. The furnishings of the entire area were rustic and lovely, like nothing I had ever seen before. There were many places to sit, to relax with others, to enjoy the view outdoors. The grand log staircase led up to the loft. I saw it beautifully decorated for fall, then Christmas. The warmth of the cozy fire filled the room.

At the far right of the great room, I saw a long, wooden table. It was massive and could seat many people. Off of the dining area, was a doorway leading to the kitchen. The kitchen had a large island countertop and I believe it had red accents and a breakfast nook tucked in the back corner.

Off of the kitchen was a hallway leading to a laundry room, a bathroom, and possibly a staircase downstairs. At the end of the hall was the entrance to another large living area. I imagined my parents were comfortable inside.

    I never saw a detailed glimpse of the downstairs. Each time I tried to see it, the Lord darkened the entryway. On a later occasion, I asked the Lord why I couldn't see that area. I felt Him saying that this area was not mine. It was a part of another's dream from Him. I thought of my eldest daughter's dedication to the elderly and my mother's love for young women experiencing crisis pregnancies. I never asked to see it again. I didn't need to know the details of another's dream. It was between them and their Lord.

    On the outside of the log lodge was countryside, pasture land, a large shop on the right, and a barn down to the left. What was behind the house was absolutely amazing. It was a camp, complete with a dining area, cabins, and a chapel. I walked inside the dining room and saw a wonderful friend of ours. He was cooking up lunch to serve to a few families that were being ministered to at the camp. Later, I saw this same man sitting at one of the tables talking to a guest. He was sharing his testimony, giving hope to one who seemed hopeless. I could see great joy and fulfillment in my friend's eyes. I remember his apron and the joy in his eyes. He felt great fulfillment in his work. This brought me joy.

    I saw the steps leading up to the chapel, but I never saw a clear glimpse of the layout inside. I haven't seen many details of the cabins either, but Greg has. The Lord showed him the construction of the buildings. It was the first vision he had of the camp. The plan was fairly simple, easy to build overall, even on a slope. He was especially excited about the handicapped accessible sites. He saw elderly couples and families with children confined to wheelchairs. He saw them enjoying an experience that they had felt excluded from.

Outside of the barn, there was a corral for exercising horses. I never saw the horses, but I knew that they were there. I knew the barn contained stalls, a hayloft, a solid roof, and electrical wiring. I imagined the patient, gentle horses who loved children and adults alike. The barn was red, with white trim.

There were also places to gather, such as an amphitheater area, a playground, and a campfire pit. I felt the glory of the Lord in worship and I saw people being set free. I felt the wind of the Holy Spirit rising on our worship. I felt joy and peace at the new found hope campers had grasped onto. Mostly, I saw entire families worshiping as one.

**Lord,**

**Thank You for showing us Your plan for our family. Thank You for making it so beautiful, so perfect for who we are in You. The work You've called us to do is not easy Lord. The people You send to us are the people much of the church has given up on, people whom You have a purpose and plan for. They are precious families and individuals who need to be set free, to learn how to rest in You, and to wait in Your presence. They are people who are discouraged, who think there is no hope, who have written off themselves and their dreams. Help**

us be ready Lord. Help us be who You have called us to be.

The Lord plans to use us to minister to people who need more than just a little encouragement. They need God to come down to them, sit with them, and do some difficult work in them that they can not do for themselves. Eagle Acres Camp will be just what the Lord ordered for them!

We call our camp 'Eagle Acres' because of Isaiah 40:31. *"But those who wait on the Lord shall renew their strength; They shall mount up with wings like eagles, They shall run and not be weary, They shall walk and not faint."* We have always seen ourselves as a refuge, a safe place for people to come, to heal, and to be restored. We see ourselves as a resting ground. We believe that God has placed this vision in us.

We feel the Lord has called us to minister to people in a camp setting. Our vision includes helping families who are struggling, working to encourage foster and adoptive families, helping people break chains such as addiction and outbursts of violence, and to help couples stay committed to their marriages. We hope to show the love of God to all He sends us. Our greatest desire is for these precious people to accept the Lord and to live for Him. Eagle Acres will be a very special place. God is going to be there with us.

As we have seen this camp with our hearts, we are more dedicated than ever to see the fulfilling of the dream. The Lord is already sending people our way who need Him desperately. Though it is sometimes easy to look only toward the future, we must focus on where the Lord has us today. We trust Him and know that He is preparing us for the days to come.

# Chapter 12

When the Lord gives you a dream, it propels you. You think about it night and day. You plan for it, write it down and meditate on what it would take to achieve it. It's hard to sleep, eat, or be satisfied with life unless you are making visible progress toward your dream. Our dreams are from the Lord.

As 2008 started, our dreams were driving us in full force. We tried to view all life changes, even those seeming like obstacles, as a step toward our dream. We felt God building our dream, right before our eyes.

Before long, our vision began to spread to our children. God spoke to some of them about the dream as well. We'd stay up late at night talking about God's plans for us. We'd get up early, excited about what the Lord might teach us that new day.

There were times when we seemed to be making mammoth progress toward our dreams. There were also times when we felt as if our dreams were on hold, because we failed to see the wisdom of the Lord. One such time started in April of 2008 when we received a telephone call asking us to care for two precious, little children.

I can not share many details as these precious children are in the state foster care system and are currently still in our care. It is important to keep their information confidential. What I can say is that an infant and a toddler joined our family. God made it very clear to us that they were to be invited into our home. A busy family of seven became a tornado of nine!

Distraction can set in when one is caring for seven children, two of whom are in diapers. Distraction can set in when one is home schooling five children. Distraction can set in when one is simply living and breathing. We have certainly experienced our share of distractions!

There were definitely times when we saw our growing family as a distraction. After a few months of parenting seven children, questions started to arise. "Lord, what is going on? What are we supposed be learning right now? Are we being tested? Are we being graded on this? Lord? Lord, are you listening to us? Lord?"

Questions are a normal part of the Christian's walk with the Lord, but so is trust, often even blind trust. We learned that what we saw as a season of distraction, the Lord, in His great wisdom, meant as preparation for a dream. The Lord is a wonderful teacher. He knows just how to get our attention, how to teach us to depend on Him, and how to prepare us for
what's ahead. We can trust the Lord's plan with reckless abandon.

*As a busy mother, I am always looking for new and creative ways to teach my children the truths of the Lord. I pray for strategy ideas and sometimes the Lord gives me some pretty crazy lesson plans! I call them Mrs. Smith's lessons from the Lord, hoping that my children will one day separate me from these crazy object lessons! These crazy ideas usually get the point across better though, than one of mom's normal, boring, long lectures.*

*One time "Mrs. Smith's" lesson from the Lord was on the importance of following rules. I was getting incredibly tired of hearing my children complain that my rules were too strict, too picky, no fun. I marched into the middle of the kitchen during breakfast and very cheerfully announced that for a few brief moments I was going to give them a reprieve of all household rules. I was setting them free of all burdensome rules for the next three minutes! My children just looked at me confused and continued eating their cereal. I had unplugged the phone and locked the doors in anticipation of total chaos.*

*"Do you understand, kids? You're free! You can do anything you want! Hurry! There's only 2 ½ minutes left!" I then stood up on a chair, carefully crawled onto the table and proceeded in spilling bowls of cereal. I picked up the napkin holder and dispensed napkins across the room. I picked up my son's medication bottle and dumped the contents onto the floor, sending little pills everywhere.*

*My youngest daughter started crying. My oldest daughter*

*chased after me cleaning up my mess. My sons stared at me horrified. I was just starting to loosen up and have some fun. The timer went off. It was time to get off the table, clean up the mess and explain to my children that there are very good reasons for the rules dad and I have set in place. Mrs. Smith has some crazy methods, but just like the Lord, she sure knows how to get our attention and make a point!*

Whatever the Lord has planned for us must be good, exciting, and challenging. He has taken some pretty extreme measures to prepare us for it! As we have prayed over our dream, shared our vision with others, and prepared for our dream's fulfillment, we have readied ourselves for a move of God. We have written our dream down, have seen visions of its reality, and have planned for its arrival. Lord, You are welcome in this place.

*We can trust the Lord's plans with reckless abandon.*

# A Season of Waiting

# Chapter 13

*Wait on the Lord; Be of good courage, and He shall strengthen your heart; wait, I say, on the Lord!* (Psalm 27:14)

When people talk to my husband and I, they often comment that we are patient people. We always laugh because we know just how impatient we usually are. Somehow we've managed to fool a few folks. Patience is definitely an area we need major improvement in.

When it comes to waiting on the Lord, we truly needed to develop our patience. For He always knows what's best and He always has perfect timing. Sometimes knowing that God is in control can be overwhelming. It's not that we desire independence. We just want to hurry up the plan, or change certain aspects of it that we are uncomfortable with. Waiting is a season that sometimes seems to last forever.

A good friend of ours spent several years desiring to get married. He watched many of his friends marry, build homes, and start families. Each passing year seemed to bring more hopelessness and discouragement. When the woman who would become his wife came along, he nearly missed the fulfillment of his dream. He was so focused on his dilemma that he failed to see the gift of the Lord before him. Our friend is now very happily married, has a young child, and knows that God had a perfect plan all the while. God's plan was worth the wait!

Sometimes we rush the Lord or even take matters into our own hands, when God has everything in and under His perfect control. Other times, we neglect to hear the voice of God telling us to move in a particular direction, therefore delaying the Lord's plans. Missing the Lord's direction can be devastating to a dream. When the Lord gives us a driving dream, we need to tend it, care for it, and nurture it. The best and only way to do this properly, is to stay as close to the Lord as possible. He understands all the details of the dream. It originated and kindled in His heart before it was ever breathed into ours. He loves us with an everlasting love. His hands are the perfect place for us and the dreams He has entrusted us with. Letting God be in total control is the only way to fulfill the dreams He has given us. Waiting on Him and waiting in Him is essential in every step of making a dream a reality.

*We have two miniature donkeys named Jack and Jill. They look like twin Eeyores from Winnie the Pooh. They're very sweet-natured and my two horse-crazy daughters have convinced them that they are royalty. They are moved to fresh pasture land each morning and are taken back to their warm stall each night. Throughout the day, they usually get a variety of apples and carrots. Once in a while, the girls even bring them their favorites, berries!*

*The problem that has recently arisen is that our two spoiled donkeys have gotten demanding and quite unthankful. They screech out their loud heehaws whenever the girls are late. They screech more when they see their snacks and the girls don't deliver them fast enough. They want their way and they want it now! When their desires are delayed, they mope and appear depressed. They refuse affection and act aloof. The worst part is that they never seem to be appreciative of their royal treatment!*

Sometimes, I'm sorry to say, we have more in common with Jack and Jill than we care to admit. We hee and haw and screech when our needs are not met in what we consider to be a timely manner. Sometimes, we see the gifts of the Lord and we feel we are entitled to them. Sometimes we even get droopy-eyed and sullen. We feel betrayed when our dreams are delayed. The truth is, sometimes we just have to wait!

As time goes on, we may have moments where we feel like the Lord has forgotten us and the dream He gave us. We might whine to the Lord so loudly that there is no wonder why He chooses to build our character and make us wait. We might forget that the Lord has always been faithful. We might forget to give Him thanks for all He has done for us. There may even be moments when we start to doubt that our dreams will ever come true. The longer we wait, the more discouragement and distraction can set in. Discouragement and distraction can kill a dream.

Not long ago, Greg and I were experiencing a time of discouragement as we waited. We stopped talking about our dreams as much and started sounding a lot more 'realistic.' Being realistic is extremely dangerous for a dreamer. Thinking logically can destroy a dream as well.

*Logically, can anyone part water or close the mouths of lions? Logically, can anyone really feed 5,000 men, plus countless women and children, with just five loaves of bread and a couple of fish? Realistically, can anyone rise from the dead or ascend into Heaven? Well, our God has done all this and much, much more! Logic and realism have no business being in the regular vocabulary of a Christian, especially a Christian with God-given dreams!*

As our discouragement grew, we eventually asked the Lord to reveal Himself to us. What did He want us to do at this point? Was our dream on hold indefinitely? The answer we received was both profound and challenging. We felt God tell us that we needed to stop whining like Jack and Jill, and start being the camp He asked us to be!

So, how do we 'be a camp?' With seven children, a couple of dogs, goats, cats, and donkeys, our lives are pretty wild. With home schooling, marriage and family ministry, Greg's job, and our family, life isn't filled with much extra time! We didn't have the time, money, or frankly, the stamina to do anything on our own. That's when we were reminded that we were NOT on our own. So, we asked the Lord for more direction and He helped us declare the first steps.

Step # 1: **Fix our thoughts.** A camp isn't just a place, it's an attitude. Our dream wasn't just some idea on paper. It was in our hearts. We looked around at the families we were currently ministering to. We discovered that each one could benefit from our camp attitude. We asked the Lord to make us Eagle Acres Camp.

Step # 2: **Declare the dream.** We had been keeping our dream to ourselves for so long, worried about people's reactions if we told them our plan aloud. What if they thought we already have too much on our plate? (thinking dangerously logically again, I'm afraid.) What if they think we're crazy for announcing something that is so far beyond what we were able to do on our own? What if God doesn't deliver and we look really, really foolish? All of these questions and more popped into our heads, but we decided to claim the truth and declare the dream for all to hear. If we proclaim that we are Eagle Acres Camp, then we are Eagle Acres Camp!

Step # 3: **Do it!** We needed to get our eyes off of our limitations, the smallness of who we are, and all that stands in-between the now and the not yet. We needed to focus on the Dream Giver! Once our focus was on the Lord, we began to see a variety of ways that we could be Eagle Acres. We could offer our home to those in need. We could start a

Saturday night 'campfire' here on our property, complete with s'mores, singing, and teaching time. We could survey the land and start blooming where we were planted.

There was much to **do** as we 'waited!'

Watching for the Lord is important, but obsessing on His next move makes our wait quite difficult. We would be much wiser to prepare ourselves as we wait. We show wisdom when we make good use of each season we are in, learning, growing, and ministering as we wait. When we are productive during our waiting, we can find joy in even the slowest of journeys.

Waiting is also much easier when we realize and accept that God is in control. Even in the most crucial ministries, God has a time line and a plan. If we let Him lead, we tell Him we trust Him and we are ready to submit to His will. If we try to take the reigns, we slow down our progress and risk jeopardizing the blessing of the Lord.

*The world tells us to 'make it happen,' God helps us to 'let it happen.' The world tells us that no help comes to those who don't help themselves.' God says that He wants to have total control.*

*We can strive and work and sweat, but if we are doing it out of the will of God, building our own empire, we will never truly succeed.*

# Chapter 14

In my attempt to be productive as I waited for the Lord, I purposed to grow in my love for Him. I purposed to spend less time seeking His hand, and more time seeking His face. The Lord drew near, for He longs to be with each of His children.

I had been praying for several months asking the Lord for a personal physical healing. Several wonderful ladies from our church prayed with me as well. I believe in healing. I believe that if God never changes, He still heals today. I also believe that God sees the whole intricate picture that our collective lives make, and He weaves His plans throughout that picture. He's the only one who sees the grand scale, and He's the only one who can possibly understand all the ripples that are created each time He does or does not intervene in our pain. I believe God desires to touch each one who has a need and perhaps He does, but just not always in the ways we would choose for Him to. As time went on, and I didn't receive relief from my need, a myriad of ideas went through my head. Was there unconfessed sin in my life that stopped my miracle? Was there an ultimate plan that would bring God more glory if I were to remain in physical pain? Was there a lack of faith on my part, or did I really believe that God could heal me? These questions replaced some of my peace with personal doubt. I was busy trying to figure out how to get my way, instead of simply letting God be God. Then I had a heart-to-heart with my Heavenly Father.

**Lord,**
**I have been seeking a miracle for quite some time. I know You can heal me, why haven't You? I need Your help Lord. I'm sorry for constantly whining about my pain. I'm sorry for questioning Your motives with me. Lord, I don't want to keep trying to pry Your hand open. I want to look into Your eyes and know that we're in unity. I want to fall deeper in love with You. I want to stop focusing on this problem, and start focusing on Your face. I love You Lord. I trust You. I want to leave this in Your hands and let You know that whatever Your reasons may be, I'm alright with them. You are God. I'm just me. I want to seek Your face Lord, not Your hands.**

My healing came soon after my change in perspective. I can't begin to understand the Lord. I can't say for certain that all children of God who pray will receive their miracles as soon as they seek the Lord, rather than His gifts, or resign themselves to His authority. This is just what happened for me. In my life, I see the Lord do amazing, wondrous things when I seek Him, before His miraculous deeds. Could it be that God desires a relationship with His children so much that He hurts when they just ask for more, rather than desire to be closer to Him or to submit to His authority? Each person can answer these questions on their own, but we have decided to seek the face of the Lord. He is everything we need and desire.

## Here I Am

*Here I am again, Dear Lord.*
*I'm so glad we're friends.*
*I've come to You so many times*
*When my ropes are at their ends.*

*Your strong arm has rescued me,*
*And when the struggles came.*
*You calmed storms and parted seas*
*When I called upon Your name.*

*But now I'm here to worship You.*
*Lord please understand.*
*For once I want to come to seek,*
*Your face and not Your hand.*

*I love Your mercy and Your grace,*
*But Lord, I long to see Your face.*
*I've come to worship You,*
*And not what You do.*

Waiting on the Lord has never been simple for us, but it is much easier when we are growing to have a deeper love for Him.

Sometimes we forget that the Lord has waited much much longer for us, than we have waited for Him. Romans 5:8 tells us *"But God demonstrates His own love toward us, in that while we were still sinners, Christ died for us."* I'm so glad that the Lord didn't give up His wait. When we start to grow impatient, we can remember that Christ had opportunities to test His patience as well, but He chose to wait for us.

*"Therefore the Lord will wait, that He may be gracious to you; And therefore He will be exalted, that He may have mercy on you. For the Lord is a God of justice; Blessed are all those that wait for Him."* Isaiah 30:18

# Chapter 15

Recently, I again asked the Lord why He wasn't moving faster on the fulfillment of the promises we felt He had given us. He led me to Joshua 18:2-3. It reads, *"But there remained among the children of Israel seven tribes which had not yet received their inheritance. Then Joshua said to the children of Israel: How long will you neglect to go and possess the land which the Lord God of your fathers has given you?"*

After reading this passage, I was immediately challenged, for my heart was flooded with the realization that at times, **I** am the one who slows the progression of my dreams. I become distracted. I get discouraged. Sometimes, simple exhaustion sets in. All of these things significantly delay me. These are seasons I choose to allow myself to experience. Sometimes a moment of grief or an episode of illness can turn into a long drawn-out season. It's sort of the equivalent of throwing myself a long pity party or grounding myself to a dungeon for an undetermined amount of time! **I**

**have the power to change my seasons.** The Lord has placed this within me. He and I, together, are unstoppable. I just keep forgetting.

*I have two daughters who are horse crazy. They read books about horses, play act that our two miniature donkeys are horses, and pray for horses each day. They also whine a great deal about the delay of their dreams.*

*As parents, we long to give our children what they wish for. We also long to see our children grow and obey. On several occasions, I have mentioned to my daughters that I would be more motivated to do what I can to help provide a horse for them when they decide to grow in responsibility. Specifically, I would like to wholeheartedly join them in praying for a horse or two, tack, and barn if I see them keep their room clean and get their chores done without my harping at them. I know God will provide.*

*My daughters are making the choice to delay their dreams. They get distracted with playing and daydreaming. In my opinion, if they really wanted horses, they would grow in responsibility. It seems so simple to me, so cut and dry.*

I am so much like my daughters. I tell the Lord that I am committed and focused on my dream, but I don't follow through on the tasks He gives me to complete. Distraction and discouragement keep me longing for things that I should be living in. It's time to change that season.

When calamity seems to surround me, it's time for a

change in perspective. It's time to put away childish things and to start living as the Lord intended me to live. It's time for a paradigm shift. For when my eyes are looking toward the Lord, I realize that all things are possible and that God is in control.

Daniel 2:20-21 says, *"Blessed be the name of God forever and ever, for wisdom and might are His. **And He changes the times and the seasons**; He removes kings and raises up kings; He gives wisdom to the wise and knowledge to those who have understanding. "*

## *With God inside me, I can change the seasons.*

# A Season of Change

# Chapter 16

I thought my book was going to end with a 'season of waiting.' I was at peace and declared myself done. Then, somewhere between editing and publishing, I messed up again. So began a brief, new season that I call deception. The Lord asked me to share it with you.

I'm still not *exactly* sure how it all happened. It was a busy time in my life. I wasn't getting enough sleep and I wasn't spending enough time with God. My life was getting more and more out of balance with each ministry opportunity that came our way. Greg and I were both noticing weariness, so we began taking turns getting the kids breakfast in the morning so that we could spend some extended quiet time with the Lord. Striving had reared it's ugly head again.

We had concluded that if we just spent more time reading the Word and praying, that we would have the extra strength we needed. Once again, we had forgotten that our strength comes from the Lord, not in our attempts to prove that we are worthy of His strength. We'll never be worthy, but

God is always gracious. Reading God's amazing Word and communicating with Him are essential in our lives, but they truly bring us life when we do them as an extension of our relationship with God, rather than as just an expression of our obedience.

I told the Lord *again* that I wanted Him to know that I was content to be wherever He wanted me, even if it meant waiting forever for our dream. I trust Him. Then, after several weeks, even months of waiting, that unquenchable stirring began again, and I became uneasy waiting. (I later came to know that stirring as the grace of God.)

I began to ask myself some difficult questions: When is waiting from God? When is waiting just crafty distraction from the enemy? When is waiting purposeful and planned by the Creator? When is waiting just a delay caused by my fears, my contentment, and even my laziness? What am I waiting for? As I asked the Lord for answers to these questions, I became surrounded by the very real, very challenging needs of the hurting. If ever there was a need for Eagle Acres Camp, it was now. Finally I asked the question that led to my breakthrough: Am I being deceived?

As I confronted the deception, the truth was revealed. You see, in my memory, I had been 'waiting.' I had completely forgotten that months earlier I had **stopped waiting** and started 'possessing the land which the Lord my God had given me!' It was as if that conversation and experience with the Lord never took place. When I thought I was waiting for God, He was actually waiting for me.

Lord,
I'm overwhelmed. There are so many hurting families that you have placed in front of us. There are huge needs that we can't begin to understand on our own. We want to help Lord, but we don't know where to begin. Please Lord, show us how to be the camp you called us to be. Help us minister to these people. Help us know how to reach them Lord. They need You so desperately. You're their only hope Lord. Help us show them who You are. Meet these needs God. We are calling out to You. We don't have time to wait Lord. We have friends who are throwing their lives away at this very moment. The enemy has them believing that they're worthless, that their pasts somehow dictate their futures. They can't wait God. Some families are literally falling apart, Lord. They're struggling with issues that I've never even been trained to deal with. I don't know where to begin to help them. We need You now, God. Tomorrow? Next year? It might be too late. We need the camp You showed us now. We need the time, the resources, the money, all of it. We need it today. We need the fresh revelation, the divine impartation, the Holy Spirit's anointing, and we need them now. These people are desperate for You, Lord. We all are. We were content to wait when things were fine. For some strange reason, we were even content to wait when things started not being fine. I deluded

**myself Lord. I was deceived and I bought it hook, line, and sinker. I thought the waiting was Your idea and now I see that somewhere along the way, You were just waiting for me. I'm not even sure just how the enemy tricked me yet, but I'm sorry Lord. I need You. Please help us be who You want us to be to help these people You sent to us. I'm tired of waiting Lord. These families can't wait Lord. The enemy has them bound, gagged, and is holding a knife to their throats. They need Your help NOW. Please. Tonight God. Tonight. Move what needs to be moved. Change, Heal, Restore, and Set Free! Please God. No more waiting.**

There are times when waiting is exactly what we're supposed to do. There are also times when waiting is just about the worst thing we could do. When we're in a season that needs to end, we can't delay. We need to stand up, repent for being calloused, indifferent, and stagnant, and CHANGE!

*If you find yourself in a rut, in a pit, in an unpleasant, ungodly mess, it's time for a change! If you find yourself in regret, in shame, in unending pain, in debt up to your neck, in fret, or in darkness, it's time for a change! If you find yourself in charge, stepped on, whomped on, or buried, it's time for a change! God wants to change your season! Don't suffer or cause further suffering any longer.*

*Bad seasons bring you pain, scar your life, and can affect your destiny.*

I knew in my heart of hearts that it was time for a change of seasons. I knew that my season of waiting was over and my season of changing was beginning. The fire in me had been rekindled. I was hungry for God because I knew I couldn't do anything without Him. I longed for Him because I knew He had the answers. I loved Him because deep inside there was hope and joy now. I had purpose.

We needed more of God! Greg and I purposed to read more of God's Word, to study the character attributes we longed to see in our lives. The first study I did was on weariness, since I often found myself being tired and weary. I relearned that my strength comes from the Lord, from putting my hope and trust in Him. (Isaiah 40:29-31) I was also reminded that when we forget our purpose, we tend to live without focus which can lead to extreme weariness. Just by lining up our vision again, my energy and stamina increased.

We also increased our communication with our Heavenly Father. Our prayer times had become quick and choppy, rather than passionate and intercessory. We had grown content in waiting and helplessness took over us. We saw a myriad of needs, but felt little ability to be able to minister to them. Somehow, during our waiting, we turned our focus from God, to our limitations. Heart-felt praying returned our focus to our Heavenly Father, removed it from us and our limitations, and ultimately gave us the power, God's power, to change lives.

Prayer changes everything. In Exodus 32, God was

going to destroy the Israelites because of their sin, but Moses intervened. He prayed, calling out to God to be merciful. God had mercy and Israel was spared. When I am content to sit back and feel powerless, I am no threat to Satan. He has me where he wants me. Many suffer. However, when I access the mighty power of God, through prayer, captives are set free. Chains are broken. Sins are forgiven, and all of Hell trembles. I can do that, simple, little me, because of the mighty power of God!

Change also comes with praise! Praise can literally revolutionize an atmosphere. Once again, our focus is taken off of ourselves and is placed where it belongs, on the King of Kings. There may be very little we can do on our own in a particular situation, but God can transform the situation, renew our minds, and can bring good from anything. (Romans 8:28) Isaiah 43:7 says that we were created to bring glory to God. When we don't praise our Lord, we cease to live out our purpose. Change is inevitable when you really cultivate it. We were so sick of what Satan was doing, that we desperately sought the Lord for change. In the midst of seeking the Lord, I found myself wondering how I had gotten to this strange, familiar place again. I looked back at my journal entries and previous seasons and discovered my answer tucked into the pages of my own book. Months before I had written,

*"Sometimes we rush the Lord or even take matters into our own hands, when God has everything in and under His perfect control.* **Other times, we neglect to hear the voice of God telling us to move in a particular direction, therefore**

*delaying the Lord's plans. Missing the Lord's direction can be devastating to a dream. When the Lord gives us a driving dream, we need to <u>tend it, care for it, and nurture it. The best and only way to do this properly, is to stay as close to the Lord as possible.</u> He understands all the details of the dream. It originated and kindled in His heart before it was ever breathed into ours."*

    We had grown cold in the Lord. We were feeling exhausted all the time. We were pushing ourselves to 'do' all the things we needed to do in our relationship with Him. We were punching in at our spiritual time clock. Somewhere during those weeks, waiting on the Lord turned into God waiting on us. He was ready to move forward. We should have seen. People were at the door, on the phone, in our pathway everywhere we went. We should have known. Instead, weary from waiting, weary from working, we were more like the 5 foolish virgins in Matthew 25:1-13, than we were like expectant believers. We had become exhausted. When it was time to be ready, we were asleep, unaware that the Lord was moving about. I'm so thankful for the grace of God.

# Chapter 17

Once we knew that God was ready to move, we were determined to see where He was going. As we prayed to know His heart, we experienced new grace. We saw God building a camp right before our eyes. It wasn't quite what we had seen in our dreams, not yet anyway. For now, we have to learn to bloom where we're planted.

Several months ago, we traveled a few hours away to pick up our camp's first two horses! They were two rescues, beautiful creatures with lots of love to give, and lots of hurts to heal. We knew they'd fit in just perfect around here! With the help of the Lord and a few good friends, we built stables over the summer. They were finished before the weather got to hot. Our camp had its critters!

*Sissy was the younger of our two horses. She was in far better shape than Jackson. She was spirited, had a healthy coat, and had experienced less trauma in her life. She was beautiful. She also died just four months after she came.*

*The vet was treating her for ulcers, but thought cancer was a possibility. The renderer suspected cancer when he picked her up after her death.*

*Our momentum was just getting started. We had been seeing so many things come together, yet we were shaken by the death of our horse. It was so much more than the loss of a beloved pet. It began a time of questioning a dream. This time never developed into a season though. We asked the Lord to draw near to us and clarify His plan.*

*When God has a plan, the enemy prepares for a counter attack. When God has a plan, the demons work overtime to see that anything discouraging that can happen will happen. God holds on to us tight but sometimes the enemy's schemes affect us. Sometimes they hinder us. We didn't let them stop us.*

*Jackson is an amazing, strong 21 year old male quarter horse. He was a rodeo champion many years ago! He worked with children and loves people of all ages. He's got lots of personality and spirit. He loves to work hard and he is becoming quite handsome! Food is his best friend right now as he has had some seasons of inconsistent care in his life. He's a gift from the Lord and we plan to share him with those the Lord sends to us.*

Next summer we're planning on building a family cabin. We have a few acres here, and we can minister to a couple of families at a time. The need is so great and we're confident that God will make a way where there seems to be no way.

Great joy has filled our hearts as our children have told us their own visions for the camp. They each have areas of ministry that the Lord has given to them and they are beginning to develop their passion for the lost. Our sweet daughters are excited about leading nature walks and teaching young people about cooking, archery, and animals. Our sons are excited about sharing life experiences, helping families understand the importance of not quitting on each other, and playing with new friends. Our children know the importance of ministering grace and mercy. They have seen God's redemption plan in action as people have changed before their eyes. They know that past hurts, failures, and patterns can be redirected and relandscaped. God can turn mourning into dancing. He can turn stumbling blocks into stepping stones. My eldest daughter, Cassy, who also has ambitions as a writer has summed it up beautifully in the following story:

### *Does the Apple Fall Far from the Tree?*
### *By* Cassidy Brie Heisler

*"Mama, does the apple fall far from the tree?" asked the curious child.*

*"No, Darling. The apple falls straight down. Sometimes it bounces and rolls, but other than that, it doesn't move far."*

*"Daddy, does the apple fall far from the tree?" questioned the child.*

*"Sweetie, of course not. The apple bounces a little*

*bit when it hits the ground, but not much more than a couple of feet."*

*"Grandpa, does an apple fall far from the tree?" then begged the child.*

*"Not usually. When the apple falls from the tree, it usually sticks into the mud or dirt and can't move any more."*

*"Grandma, does the apple fall far from the tree?" pleaded the child.*

*"Probably not Baby. It doesn't have two legs like us to walk with."*

*God, does an apple fall far from the tree?" cried the child.*

*"Come with Me. Let's go and see." God took the child's tiny hand tenderly in His own, clasping it lovingly.*

*"God, my mama, daddy, grandma, and grandpa all say the apple doesn't fall far from the tree, but I just don't know."*

*God took the small child over to a beautiful apple tree and pointed it out. "Now look here Precious. Do you see any other apple trees near this one?"*

*"No," wondered the child.*

*"Well, if apples never fell far from the tree, how come there aren't more apple trees close by?" The child looked at the Master in wonder. "You see, My child, birds, deer, and bears eat these apples and scatter the seeds every which way. The winds come from the North and East and blow the seeds farther still. Even the simplest rain storm can carry the apples down the hill, toward the river, and far away from the tree that gave them life."*

*"Thank you God for showing me all of this."*
*"You're welcome."*
*Happily, the child scurried away to let everyone know the truth. As God watched the child walking in the light, He couldn't help but smile.*

So many times in life, we let our past define us. We let our fears stop us. We let our seeds take root right where we have landed, even if it's under a tree that we grew up promising God and ourselves we'd walk away from one day. Change is seldom easy and comfortable, but when the Holy Spirit leads it, it is always beneficial for the believer and for the Kingdom of God.

When I look back and wonder how Satan was able to deceive me those weeks ago, I now realize a few important things. First of all, I open myself up to weakness when I let myself grow too tired or weary.

*When I was a Junior in Bible College, it was an incredibly busy year. I was working off campus, on campus, attending class full time, and was involved in several challenging ministries. During a morning class, a particularly small class, I accidentally fell asleep one day. I remember waking with a startled expression and the professor gently looking at me saying, "Honey you're obviously exhausted. Get the notes from someone after class and get some rest. I really don't mind." I was mortified and never fell asleep in his class again, thinking that his direct dialogue was a great cure to my inattentiveness. Many years later, however, I have come to realize that this dear man of God probably meant exactly what he said. For when we are exhausted, we are vulnerable and we are weak.*

    I have also realized that I need to kindle the flame of the Lord. I believe we all go through what I refer to as 'valley times,' where we don't sense the presence of the Lord as strong as other times in our lives. However, I also know that God is always near to us and longs to have a close relationship with us. Close relationships take work. They take dedication and commitment. They take shared passion. If I want that kind of relationship with my Lord, I need to tend the flame, not just rely on the coals, for when I have a heart that is on fire for God I am less likely to listen to the deceptive, wooing words of the enemy. When I lack the strength to go to God, I must remember that He never lacks the strength to come to me.

    Another realization that I have come to know is that God has an intense love for each of the families that He wants us to minister to, but Satan has an intense hatred for them. Satan wants to destroy them, not to see them restored and healed. He'll go to great lengths to stop or delay the work of God. He knows that in deceiving me, he disarms a powerful opponent. We need to be on guard at all times, for the enemy is crafty and deceitful. There is nothing evil he wouldn't do. On the other hand, God is loving, kind, and gracious. To His mercy, there is no end. We defeat the enemy by simply remembering where to keep our focus! Focusing on God keeps our eyes off of the enemy! Focusing on God brings about the changes that need to come.

# Chapter 18

Some books are intentionally written with the author setting up the readers for the sequel. It was never my purpose to create a work that was only partially complete, but my life, my seasons, can only be complete when I meet my Lord in Heaven. Even then, though, my season in eternity will have just begun unraveling, for some seasons are never meant to end.

As I live out each ensuing day, filling in the next lines of the next chapters, I will be praying for you. I will be praying that your seasons are the seasons that God wants you in, that those who need change will let God change the course of their journeys. I pray that friends who find themselves in difficult, painful seasons will know for certain that God is with them, loves them, and never seeks to harm them. I pray that those who are waiting will let the Lord help them discern if they are waiting on Him or if He is waiting for them. I pray that those who are in healthy, wonderful seasons, will find the strength and inspiration to nurture them, value them, and help them flourish.

The seasons I have left to live are as much a mystery to me as they are to you. Please forgive me for leaving the rest of story untold. I simply cannot do any better. I would like to say that I have worked out all of my kinks and shortcomings and that I will never lose my focus on God again. I say this with tears in my eyes because the pain of my recent deception is fresh. I would like to say that every season I walk through will be pleasant from now on, because I have learned enough to avoid the hard seasons and I am intelligent enough to lean on the Lord at all times. The truth is though, that I mess up frequently. I falter sometimes. I still get distracted by my own ideas. They seem wise to me, until the Lord shows me that my thinking is foolishness. I have so far to go, and the Lord knows what seasons will best get me there. Today, it's all about change! Tomorrow? Only the Lord knows.

What I do know is this: He who began a good work in me will be faithful to complete it. (Philippians 1:6) I can do all things through Christ who strengthens me. (Philippians 4:13) If I seek God, I will find Him, if I seek Him with all of my heart. (Jeremiah 29:13)

**Lord,
as I go on my way, continuing my journey with You, please help me not to lose sight of these things I've learned. These seasons have been precious to me, Lord, for they have drawn me closer to You. You have held me so close, helped me through so**

much, and taught me things I never could have learned on my own. Thank You for intervening Lord. Thank You for not giving up on me. As we embark on whatever the future holds, please know that I trust You with my life, my family, my dreams, all my seasons. I love You, Lord.

## Conclusion

*"There is a time for everything, a season for every activity under Heaven. A time to be born and a time to die. A time to plant and a time to harvest. A time to kill and a time to heal. A time to tear down and a time to rebuild. A time to cry and a time to laugh. A time to grieve and a time to dance. A time to scatter stones and a time to gather stones. A time to embrace and a time to turn away. A time to search and a time to lose. A time to keep and a time to throw away. A time to tear and a time to mend. A time to be quiet and a time to speak up. A time to love and a time to hate. A time for war and a time for peace."* **(NLT)** Ecclesiastes 3:1-8

Life is made of different seasons. Some seasons we go through are short and sweet. Others are long, drawn out, and difficult. Whatever season we are in, it's best to learn all we can in it. What season are you in right now? Are you struggling through a season of loneliness or a season of doubt? Are you flying high in a season of faith and expectancy? Perhaps you are facing a season of rigorous testing or a season of great blessing. You may even be going through various seasons simultaneously. Whatever the case may be, God is with you in each season, and if you ask Him, He'll help you grow in it.

    Some of the seasons we face, are seasons that the Lord has placed us in. Other times in our lives are related to choices we have made on our own. We can be sure that our Heavenly Father is alive and well and that He is active in every season we face. When we bring a difficult season upon ourselves, with the poor choices we make, we need to realize that wise, Godly choices can change our season yet again. We also need to realize that even traumatic, painful times in our lives can be used by the Lord as a growing, strengthening, character building time. God can use any season for His glory.

*As I write, my heart knows that a painful season is ahead for me and my family. The little ones we have been fostering for over a year and a half will be going home soon. The babies I have loved, the precious little ones who have called me Mommy, need to go back now. Though their reunion with their birth family is exactly what I have prayed for, I have to admit that my heart is breaking. There is no real way to explain to these children that I am not abandoning them.*

*Though I do have to walk through this season, I don't have to walk through it alone. Though I realize it's going to hurt, I don't have to die in it. I can choose to keep my eyes on my Lord, cling to Him for comfort, and grow. I can choose to invite a trusted friend or two into my pain. I know now that by telling them I am hurting, I am strengthening our friendship. I am so grateful for the grace and mercy of the Lord. His comforting arms will not only get us through this time, it will spur us on to greater things.*

 It's easy to recognize what seasons we have gone through after the season is over. It takes a great deal of self-awareness and reflection, however, to distinguish the seasons we are going through right now. It's easy for many of us to sit back and let life happen to us. It takes courage to recognize and confess that we are heading down a path, going through a season, that we know is not what the Lord wants. We must boldly let the Lord change our course in order to experience the peace and blessings that He desires to give.

 A few moments ago, I asked you what season you were in right now. Perhaps a better question would be, 'What season does the Lord desire for you right now?' Is it time to turn and face a different direction? Is it time to find joy right where you're planted, in the season you're in? Is it time to trust the Lord for a complete revolution of your heart and attitude? Ecclesiastes 3:1 says that there is a time, a season, for all things. Is your time line in line with the Lord's?

 I've seen some rough seasons in my lifetime. I've experienced some trials that have brought on seasons that were long and hard. I have also experienced the blessing and the presence of the Lord. The past is the past though. I now look toward the many seasons ahead. I don't know all that the Lord has planned for me in the days to come, but I do know that God is always, has always, and always will be faithful. He is perfect and He has me in His hands. My future is good.

When the Lord asked me to write this book, it was clear that it was to be called, <u>Seasons</u>. I believe that if we look at our life in seasons, we can find meaning in wherever we may be. Whether the season is short, long, brought on by us, brought on by the Lord, enjoyable, or challenging, it is our season. We can decide to grow in it or complain about it. We can decide to wallow in it or learn from it. We can decide to continue in it or to let the Lord end it. We can go through times of Winter, Spring, Summer, or Fall as long as we walk hand-in-hand with the Lord.

It is my hope that every season you find yourself in draws you nearer to the Lord. It is my wish that you are challenged to let the Lord chart the direction of your journey. It is my desire that you learn and grow in each place you find yourself, and that you recognize that the Lord desires to lead you!

# Afterword

I just finished canning 8 quarts of applesauce! We froze about 12 more. The kids, Grandma Pat, and I were all huddled around the table peeling, coring, and slicing until late in the evening! Monroe was so wonderful to invite us out to glean whatever we could use from his orchard. I think we might try drying some apple slices in the dehydrator this weekend. The kids said they loved the smell of the apples and cinnamon as they went to bed! As for me, it's so much more!

I photographed pictures of the orchard yesterday, wondering about the life cycle of the trees, daydreaming about the day the Lord sent my apples. I chose a couple of perfect looking beauties still on the tree for my book cover and cell phone screen! I blogged about the trip to the orchard. I took lots of photos of the kids surrounded by the trees that the Lord's apples came from. Greg looked at me smiling a few times and I knew he knew. I was fantasizing about God again. God heard me. He loves me. I'm significant. It happened for me all over again! My apple shaped love letters from the Lord are filling up 2 big boxes in the Greg's shop! I'm even sharing them with the donkeys!

**Thank You Lord. Thank You.**

*Contact Us*

Roxanne Meeuwsen, MA

Seasonsbook@gmail.com

www.Seasonsbook.blogspot.com

# COMING SOON
## from Eagle Acres Ministries:

# Whatever It Takes: A Stubborn Love
### New book coming in Spring 2010

## Our Vision

*"But those who wait on the Lord shall renew their strength; They shall mount up with wings like eagles, They shall run and not be weary, They shall walk and not faint."* Isaiah 40:31

Eagle Acres is a place of restoration. We minister to individuals, couples, and families that need to find rest, strength, and the courage to persevere. Eagles Acres is a place of refuge, a place to discover the grace and power of God, and a place to find healing. We believe that God works powerfully in the dynamics of the family. We believe in unconditional love, stubborn commitment, and in reliance on God's word. We believe prayer changes all things and that God loves each person He created with a devotion we can't begin to understand. Eagle Acres is a place to rest in the Lord, to pursue His ways, and to spark and kindle the dreams He has for us.

Visit us at **www.Seasonsbook.blogspot.com**